CCSS **Genre** Realistic Fic

MW00570372

Essential Question
What can learning about different cultures
teach us?

All the Way from Europe

by Hugh Brown
illustrated by Nick Hardcastle

CHAPTER 1
No More Old Buildings!

Sarah turned off the TV and sighed. "They sound like they're speaking another language," she said.

Her mom laughed, "They're speaking French!"

"I know," Sarah smiled. Back in North Carolina, Sarah had been excited about coming to Europe. Her mom had some work to do there, and they planned to go sightseeing together when she had free time.

However, after these first two days in Paris, Sarah was already starting to get bored. Why were adults so interested in old buildings?

Sarah wished she'd brought her saxophone to practice. Her mom had said it would be too loud.

That afternoon, they drove to Brussels, a city in Belgium. Sarah tried reading a guidebook, but it was all about old buildings! She closed the book and sighed again.

"Enough fun for today?" her mother asked.

Sarah said, "Not really," looking sad and **glum**.

"How about this? When we get to a new city, you can use my laptop to **research** things to do. Then, when I finish my work in the morning, we'll do what you want in the afternoon. Deal?"

STOP AND CHECK

Why is Sarah feeling unhappy?

Sarah thought for a moment. Then she said, "I must **congratulate** you on a great idea."

"Are you **complimenting** me? Careful, or I'll get too proud of myself!" her mom laughed.

Sarah grinned. "So tell me, why did they name a city after Brussels sprouts?"

Her mom said, "You'll have to look it up."

STOP AND CHECK

Why does Sarah's mother suggest a new plan?

CHAPTER 2

Saxophones and Hotdogs

The next day, Sarah's mom finished her work before lunch. "What are we doing this afternoon?" she asked.

"Well," Sarah said, "two of my favorite things come from here. First, Brussels sprouts."

"But you don't like Brussels sprouts."

"Got you!" Sarah **blurted** out. "I learned that the city isn't named after Brussels sprouts. The sprouts are named after the city because they were first grown here."

"So what are your real favorite things from here?" asked her mom.

"The Tintin stories," said Sarah. "A Belgian author wrote them. There's even a museum here about comics. That's my kind of **cultural** museum."

"You know I love the saxophone," Sarah continued. "Well, the man who invented it was born near Brussels. The Museum of Musical Instruments has a collection of his instruments, and lots of fun, hands-on stuff to do."

Her mother looked disappointed. "That sounds good," she said, "but ..."

Sarah laughed, "Don't worry. I didn't forget about Belgian chocolate. We're also going to the Museum of Cocoa and Chocolate."

Her mom brightened up. "Perfect!"

Next, Sarah and her mom visited Frankfurt in Germany. Sarah's mom asked, "So what's our plan today?"

"There's a **communication** museum that looks interesting," she replied. "They have old telephones and televisions. And then we'll go eat hotdogs."

"But shouldn't we try some German food?" asked her mom.

"The frankfurter comes from Frankfurt," explained Sarah. "The German people took them to New York and sold them in buns. That's when people began calling them hotdogs."

"Okay. Let's go eat some frankfurters!" said her mom.

STOP AND CHECK

What did Sarah find out about Brussels and Frankfurt?

CHAPTER 3

Don't Eat the Hamburgers!

Sarah and her mom set off to the next city in Germany, which was called Hamburg. On the way, Sarah saw a sign that said "Bremen."

"Where have I heard the name Bremen before?" she asked.

"It's from a story called *The Musicians of Bremen.* I used to read it to you," her mom said.

"Oh! I remember now," Sarah said. "I loved that story."

She looked out the window. They were passing another town. "Remember when we looked at the map back home? I thought it would take a long time to get to a different country, but the countries here are small **compared** with the United States."

"It shows you how huge the United States is," her mother said. "The United States is a bit like Europe. The different states are like the different countries of Europe."

"When you think of it like that," said Sarah, "it's no surprise that the states are so different from each other."

"You've learned something about home while you've been in Europe," her mom **commented**. "So, what will we see in Hamburg?"

"We are going to visit the zoo and then we can look at the Hamburgers in town," said Sarah.

"And let's eat the hamburgers after we look at them," said her mom.

"No! We can't eat them!" Sarah **contradicted**.

"Why not?" her mom asked.

"Hamburgers are the people who live in Hamburg," Sarah explained. "The hamburgers we eat were probably named after the meat patties that German immigrants ate in the United States."

Sarah's mom looked **relieved**. "Whew! I can relax now. So then let's look at Hamburgers while we eat American-style hamburgers."

"Yes!" Sarah laughed.

STOP AND CHECK

What does Sarah do to learn about Hamburg?

CHAPTER 4
Pizza and Soccer

Sarah and her mom spent two days in Hamburg, and then they flew to Naples, in Italy.

At the hotel, Sarah took out the laptop to start her research.

Sarah's mom smiled. "I think you enjoy this research. And maybe it is giving you a new **appreciation** of home."

Sarah nodded. "When we get home, I'm going to do research on North Carolina. There must be lots I don't know."

The next morning while Sarah's mom worked, Sarah looked out the window, watching people on the street.

Finally, her mom finished. "What are we doing today?"

"We're eating Neapolitan pizza!" Sarah said. "Neapolitan means 'from Naples,' and Naples is famous for pizza."

"Pizza is your favorite food. There's another fact!" laughed her mother.

They walked to a pizzeria, ordered a pizza, and then sat at a table outside. Across the road, a group of kids was playing soccer. Sarah wished she could join their game.

Sarah's thoughts were **interrupted** by the waiter bringing the pizza. Her mom whispered, "Was there a **misunderstanding**? Is this pizza?"

Sarah giggled. "I think so. Doesn't it smell **delicious**?"

"I'm not trying to be **critical**," commented Sarah's mom, "but the crust is so thin you can barely find it under the cheese!"

After eating, they walked to the park. A boy playing soccer missed a pass, and the ball rolled toward Sarah. She kicked it back to him, and he called out, *"Grazie!"* Sarah knew that meant "thank you." Then the boy called out something else in Italian.

"I don't speak Italian," Sarah called. The boy came over.

"Are you from England?" he asked in English.

"I'm American," Sarah said.

"Would you like to play soccer with us?" he asked.

"I'd love to!" she said. She looked at her mom, who nodded yes.

The boy said, "I didn't know Americans played soccer. How did you learn?"

"It's like the saxophone, hotdogs, and pizza," Sarah explained. "They were all brought to America and then they became some of our favorite things."

STOP AND CHECK

What does Sarah learn in Naples?

Summarize

Summarize the important details in *All the Way from Europe*. Your graphic organizer may help you.

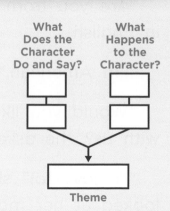

What Does the Character Do and Say?

What Happens to the Character?

Theme

Text Evidence

1. Reread Chapter 3. What do Sarah and her mom learn about the United States? How does this show the author's main message? **THEME**

2. Find the word *sightseeing* on page 2. What does *sightseeing* mean? Use clues from the text to help you figure it out. **VOCABULARY**

3. How did Sarah's feelings change after Chapter 1? Write about how this change helps show the author's message.
   WRITE ABOUT READING

Compare Texts

Read about where some sports started.

A SPORTING GIFT

Many sports that we think are American came from other places.

AMERICAN FOOTBALL

Some people say that modern American football began in England in 1823. A boy named William Ellis was playing soccer when he picked up the ball and ran with it! That was the beginning of a game called rugby. Rugby players can carry and throw the ball. Over time, the rugby ball became oval-shaped because that made it easier to carry and pass than a round ball.

In the 1870s, American football was more like soccer than like rugby. Then schools began to let players carry and throw the ball. These rules were popular by the 1880s. American football had begun.

Baseball started out as an English children's game called "rounders." Rounders is played with a round bat and four bases. English immigrants brought this game to the United States, where it slowly changed.

Some people think that an American named Abner Doubleday "invented" baseball in 1839. But it is more likely that the rules of modern baseball were first written down in the 1840s in New York. Members of a "base ball" team there wrote down the "New York rules." These became the rules of baseball today.

Basketball was invented in 1891 by an American named James Naismith. He wanted to create a fun indoor game that would keep people in shape in the winter. Many of the rules Naismith made are part of the game today.

The game was called "basket ball" because the first hoops were baskets used to store peaches. Every time a goal was scored, someone had to climb a ladder to get the ball! Later, players used nets. Basketball is now played all around the world.

Make Connections

What does soccer have in common with American football? ESSENTIAL QUESTION

How do *All the Way from Europe* and *A Sporting Gift* show the way that things and ideas travel around the world? TEXT TO TEXT

Focus on
Literary Elements

Dialogue Dialogue shows readers what characters say. Dialogue can help move the plot along. It can also show action. Think about how a comic strip tells a story. It uses only dialogue and illustrations.

Read and Find Look at page 14. In this piece of dialogue, the author tells us what the characters say and what they are doing. What kinds of pictures could help tell the story?

Her mom whispered, "Was there a misunderstanding? Is this pizza?"

Sarah giggled, "I think so. Doesn't it smell delicious?"

"I'm not trying to be critical," commented Sarah's mom, "but the crust is so thin you can barely find it under the cheese!"

Your Turn

Turn this dialogue into a comic strip. Write the words the characters say. Add your own drawings. Work with a partner or on your own. Show your comic strip to your classmates.